# YOU CAN TEACH
# Primaries

## ELSIEBETH McDANIEL

Updated, expanded from
*There's More to Teaching Primaries*

How to gain insights into teaching children
and leading them to love the Lord

## VICTOR BOOKS

a division of SP Publications, Inc.
WHEATON, ILLINOIS 60187

*Offices also in* Fullerton, California • Whitby, Ontario, Canada • Amersham-on-the-Hill, Bucks, England

ISBN: 0-88207-143-2

VICTOR BOOKS
A division of SP Publications, Inc.
P.O. Box 1825  •  Wheaton, Illinois 60187

# CONTENTS

# to
# every Primary
# Sunday School
# teacher

The author, Elsiebeth McDaniel, holds a B.A. and M.A. from Wheaton College. She is Director of Early Childhood Publications at Scripture Press. She has authored several books, including *You and Children,* and *You and Preschoolers,* with Lawrence O. Richards. She has worked with Primaries in Sunday School, Children's Church, Vacation Bible School, and weekday clubs.

# 1
# You Can
# Be a Teacher!

Welcome to the wonderful world of Primaries! Theirs is a world filled with movement, discovery, laughter, and action! It's an exciting world, and you can become a part of it as you become involved in listening to Primaries—giving assurance to the timid, helping children discover, sharing Bible truths, and showing respect for children and their ideas. You will communicate with Primaries without talking down. You will teach children how to think without teaching them what to think. And sometimes the Lord may allow you to be the one who will introduce a young child to the Saviour—God's wonderful Son Jesus Christ.

If the Lord has called you to be a teacher in the Primary department, obey Him, for He has said, "Teach all!" (Matthew 28:19-20) Furthermore, the Lord will carry the larger part of the responsibility for reaching boys and girls with His Word, for He loves them and knows each one intimately. As you become the instrument through which the Holy Spirit will work, you'll find that boys and girls grow in their Christian faith, sometimes in giant steps and sometimes in weak, wavering, footsteps—just as you and I have grown and continue to grow.

Yes, be a teacher! "And they that be wise shall shine as the brightness of the firmament; and they that turn many to righteousness as the stars forever and ever" (Daniel 12:3).

Commitment, determination, and love are needed, but what else?

Some practical know-how! This book will help you see what you need to be and do to effectively teach to the glory of God! Sometimes teachers do an inadequate job of teaching because they do not sense the responsibility that the Lord has given them. A teacher is not an entertainer—or someone to "keep the kids quiet." You are an "under shepherd"—one of the few Christians in your community who is interested in the spiritual growth of a particular group of children.

Mrs. Smith, a sincere Christian who loved children, got up early every Sunday morning to study her lesson. She tried to remember all the details. But in class her children did not seem interested. She found it difficult to get their attention and keep it on the lesson truth.

Knowing the Lord, studying His Word, and loving the children are all necessary, but it is also imperative to prepare thoroughly. Sunday morning is a poor time to prepare for Sunday teaching!

Long before you plan for your class, do you prepare your own heart? Do you spend time in *daily* prayer for your pupils? Take a photograph of your class. Then post it where you will see it every day. Pray for individuals—not just the class. Do you ask the Lord to teach *you* through the Bible passage, or do you concentrate on what the children should learn according to the manual?

After the Lord has spoken to a teacher, that teacher is incapable of beginning with, "Let's see, today our lesson is about. . . ." Instead, he or she can scarcely wait to share God's truth with children. The prepared teacher has consistently dedicated his teaching to the Lord, continually prayed for guidance from the Holy Spirit, and consciously planned to have his pupils know, feel, and do something about each lesson.

What a tremendous responsibility a teacher has—to teach an immortal soul to enjoy fellowship with God! But to do this, *you* must be wholly dedicated to the Lord and to the task He has for you.

## Who is a Christian?

Because one purpose for this book is to help teachers lead children to Jesus Christ, it is important that every reader knows what it means to be a Christian. What are the distinguishing marks of a Christian? Teachers are Christians because of what they believe, and they are recognized as Christians by what they say and do.

It is not enough to know that God sent His Son to be the Saviour of the world; a teacher must personally trust Jesus to be his or her personal Saviour. God's Word explains the need for a Saviour:

> "They are all under sin . . . there is none righteous, no not one" (Rom. 3:9-10).

God tells us in His Word that the Saviour is His Son, the only Saviour, and how to receive Him:

> "But God commendeth His love toward us, in that, while we were yet sinners, Christ died for us" (Rom. 5:8).

> "For whosoever shall call upon the name of the Lord shall be saved" (Rom. 10:13).

> "For God so loved the world, that He gave His one and only Son, that _____ (fill in your name) [who] believes in Him shall not perish, but have eternal life" (John 3:16, NIV).

A Christian teacher recognizes that he is not righteous of himself. He knows that Christ died for his sin. He has called on the name of the Lord, believing Him to be his Saviour from sin and Lord of his life.

## You may as well know . . .

Often a workshop leader begins a session by asking teachers what they like about teaching and what bothers them. If you are a beginning teacher, you may as well know ahead of time that some things will bother you. If you are an experienced teacher, you will be encouraged to know that all teachers like some aspects of teaching Primaries, but are bothered by some things.

"What bothers me," said one teacher, "are the children who keep coming late week after week."

Another quickly added, "It isn't those who come late. It's the kids who get there long before I'm organized and ready for them." What answers will you find in this book for these two problems?

Other Primary workers talk about classroom clowns, dreary rooms, and the seeming lack of appreciation. Perhaps some of these are your problems.

But there's another side to teaching Primaries—the things teachers like! "I'm so glad I kept on teaching first-graders! I was about to give up, but last week one of the boys received Christ as his Saviour." Another teacher commented, "I just love Primaries. They like you and let you know it."

Do these comments sound like yours? How should you change your teaching to overcome your problems? Do you think you're really making life-lasting impressions?

For example, one Primary teacher worked till late at night in making paper-bag puppets and scenery. Then she felt foolish in presenting the stories. The children just looked and did not seem to respond. However, about 12 years after those teaching sessions, the teacher received a note from a young woman who was planning to teach in a Christian school. She had been looking everywhere for that set of puppet stories because they had meant so much to her as a Primary child. Yes, Teacher, a great deal can be accomplished through your teaching; and perhaps the old phrase "only eternity will show the results" is more true than we think!

## How do you look?

Even if some of the lessons you teach are forgotten, your life—the real you—is remembered. Your appearance is the first thing your pupils see. It is part of your identity. "The child who identifies with his teacher through affection, admiration, and submissiveness will 'take unto himself' not only what the teacher believes and teaches but also what he is and does."[1]

You are a living model of what you hope your pupils will become. While the children may evaluate your appearance first, because it is easily seen, they will also feel your love and concern for them. Physical appearance is important, and you'll want to do something about evaluating your own.

Are your pupils unable to "hear" you because of physical mannerisms—gestures or facial movements? Do you constantly tug at your clothing, jewelry, or hair? Other distractions may include a piece of clothing that does not stay in place, such as a tie. Drab colors

---

[1]Lawrence O. Richards, *Creative Bible Teaching,* page 181.

may make your subject seem drab, too. A favorite kindergarten teacher always chooses some clothing with the colors that will appeal to her pupils. If you wear a hat or other outdoor clothing in Sunday School, your children may wonder if you are cold or perhaps do not intend to stay. Your clothing should not be overly casual, but it should help children feel at ease.

Of course, more of you shows than outward appearance. Children seem able to read emotions, attitudes, and relationships. These are areas where a child can see evidence of the faith you are trying to practice and teach. The child must find you to be an attractive example of the way of life you recommend, or he may not even be

tempted to follow it. If a child likes what he sees in you, he will listen to what you have to say. He will offer his friendship and good behavior in response to your friendship and the high expectation he senses you have for him. A nine-year-old boy paid the highest of all compliments to his teacher when he said, "He's not a teacher; he's a friend!"

What characteristics are important in a Primary teacher? Here are some that boys and girls think are very important. Notice how many involve loving the children.

1. A good teacher has a pleasant voice.

2. A good teacher knows the names of his pupils—nobody wants to be "what's his name" or "the girl in blue."

3. A good teacher knows what he is doing.

4. A good teacher is emotionally well-balanced and has a pleasant disposition—smiles a lot.

5. A good teacher has a cooperative, democratic attitude; is kind and considerate of the individual.

6. A good teacher is not overly permissive, but is dedicated to doing the best for his pupils because he loves each child.

7. It has been said, "A good teacher does not push children around, but neither does he let them fool around."

For Primaries, you are the Sunday School—at least 90% of it. The teacher who can show forth Christ will have most or all of the following characteristics:

1. Has a vital relationship with the Lord.

2. Loves children and is concerned about them—not only in class, but throughout the week.

3. Is enthusiastic about the Lord, life, and lessons.

4. Uses effective learning tools as a result of creative planning.

5. Has self-confidence because he knows he is called of God and sustained by God.

## So what is a good teacher?

The teacher's example either contradicts or emphasizes, adding exclamation points to what he teaches. This important chapter about being a teacher is placed first in the book because unless you are willing to work at being an effective teacher, there is little point in studying children, how they learn, or how you can best teach them. Yes, you are more important than methods.

Doesn't everything about being a good teacher boil down to this: We all like the teacher who treats us as a *person*. But be careful that you do not place a child's opinion of you, wanting to be liked by the child, above your own standard of excellence. For example, any teacher who measures his teaching ability in terms of student popularity may be in for a shock. Primaries will love you while you are their teacher, but come next year, they may not even remember your name. The typical Primary is completely taken up with his current teacher. Nevertheless you have made your mark on his life if you have taught for the glory of God.

You'll want to be a good teacher, but that does not mean that you are a perfect person. John Holt says in his book, *How Children Fail,* that adults are not always honest about themselves—their fears, limitations, weaknesses, prejudices, and motives. Some teachers present themselves to children as if they were perfect—all-knowing, all-powerful, always rational, always just, and always right. This is the worst lie any teacher can tell about himself. Let the children know you have learned and you are still learning.

Have you enough faith in God to be honest with your boys and girls? Do you think that if you show any human tendencies you will destroy their faith? You won't. They will see you as a real person who is still learning to trust God.

Work at your teaching ministry as earnestly as you would at a secular career. Be diligent in God's work for it is a high and holy ministry.

# To think about

1. Write your description of an ideal teacher.

2. Are you strong enough for some self-examination? Be conscious of smiling the next time you teach. How did you do? Tape-record your story and listen to the tape. Ask a fellow teacher to critique your appearance.

3. Decide on one specific change you will make about yourself or your teaching technique. Then work at it.

# 2
# You Can
# Understand Children!

The 20th century has been called "the century of the child." A great deal has happened to help children, though there is still more we need to do to alleviate child abuse, malnutrition, and exploitation in some areas. What has happened in this century for children? In the first decade or two graded curriculum materials were introduced, built on the conviction that children's needs and abilities are different at various ages.

In succeeding decades, medicine accomplished much in treating childhood diseases. The fine arts were opened to children in ways never permitted previously. John Dewey, Arnold Gesell, Erik Erikson, Jean Piaget, and other theorists worked hard at understanding children. Perhaps the one important principle they all share is that human growth is best described in developmental terms. In other words, as persons mature, the changes that take place occur in an orderly fashion, each building on the last. Though the rate of growth varies among children, we have learned that the sequence or pattern of change remains the same. Because we are beginning to understand this developmental process of growth, we can make some general statements about children. At the same time, we must recognize individual differences.

As a teacher of Primaries, you need to know some general things about the development of children between the ages of six to eight or nine. Then, in addition, you will want to be sensitive to the needs of the particular group of children you are teaching.

Many things about Primaries are the same today as they were 50 years ago. Other things are not the same. How is today's child different from one living in the pre-Space Age and the pre-Electronic Age? Do you know Primaries who know more about political situations and power in the world than you did at the same age?

In looking at a boy or girl, we need to think of the whole child—the emotional, physical, social, intellectual, and spiritual growth. This has been described as a "wholistic" approach and is necessary because physical development often influences social growth. Emotional problems—such as moving to a new community—may have a direct effect on a child's desire to achieve at school. In your teaching of Primaries, try to see the whole child and his life apart from Sunday School.

Is growing up work? Yes, it is, requiring a great deal of energy to develop from a helpless infant to a well-developed adolescent. Primary teachers are meeting children who have developed large-muscle skills—running, jumping, kicking, throwing—to say nothing of noise-making. Many children bring these skills to Sunday School, to the dismay of their teachers. Why not recognize that these are achievements for the child? We'll not encourage an overuse of these skills, but find better ways to channel this bursting energy into significant learning. By Primary years this high level of energy can be redirected into enthusiasm for learning new things and working on projects.

In recent years some parents, educators, and other adults have become very interested in a child's self-identification. We hear and read a great deal about the importance of a child's self-image. This is all part of growing up. A child moves from identity with a parent figure to his self-identity. Primaries are still finding out who they are and what they can do. Your respect for a child and his thoughts, as well as your love, can be an important factor in developing a child's self-image. We need to think to ourselves and perhaps on occasion say to a child, "There's just one person in this whole world like you— and I like you just the way you are." Try it.

Who are the children *you* teach? Have you thought of *your* Primaries as individuals—each uniquely himself? Do you realize that what you teach these children helps set the child's understanding and acceptance of values and attitudes? Perhaps right now we need to remember that teaching is not effective till pupils have learned. This fact will be explained in detail in the next chapter, "How do children learn?"

How will understanding the age-level characteristics of your children help you? When is it also important to know something of a child's family life? What should you know about each child's world— his friends, school, experiences, and interests?

The child you teach may be "Sunday's child" to you, but your teaching should make an impact on his life Sunday through Saturday. Because this is true, you need to know where and how each child is living—not merely a physical location, but the many influences that affect him. Until you know something of what is going on in the minds and emotions of your pupils, you will have difficulty in making contact with them. When you know your pupils' experiences, concerns, and problems, you can—through the power of the Holy Spirit—make the Bible real to them.

## How are today's children different?

The technology of today makes many differences in learning, entertainment, and attitudes. But in addition, children seem to be living under greater pressures than ever before. Some of these points of stress are caused by family life, pressure to achieve, physical limitations—an active child being forced to live in a crowded apartment with not enough space for large-muscle activity—and living in a thought world of violence brought about by watching and believing some television programs. Because of the declining birthrate, many children lack friends. A child may be the only one in his family and perhaps the only child in the neighborhood. Today's children are often being raised in nurseries and day-care facilities. During their free time, worried mothers cart them from one organized activity to another so the children don't become bored or feel lonely.

Primaries are spending more time with their parents and less time with their friends, making them more competitive and less imaginative. Members of today's "lonely generation" are brighter and more

talented, perhaps, than their parents were, but also more selfish and high-strung. One Christian psychiatrist believes that between 6 and 10 percent of today's children are hyperactive. Some of your children may be "latch-key" youngsters who come home after school to a place with no parent present.

You can watch children; and you can teach children. Is there any other way to better understand them? Yes, listen, listen, *listen!* Each child is unique and is living in a world that may be vastly different from the world of your childhood. Use the following seven points to recall your childhood and compare it with that of some of your Primaries.

1. What did you think about the future when you were a child? A few generations ago children could visualize their future adulthood from watching grandparents. Now change is so great and frequent that the future is literally unknown.

2. There are few absolutes in today's culture. Several solutions may be taught as ethically right, though one may be better than others. But the gray area of choice seems to grow larger as the areas of what's wrong and what's right seem to shrink. Why is cheating wrong? The average Primary will explain that cheating is wrong because he might copy the wrong answer, not because cheating is a form of stealing.

The stability of home, church, and school formerly helped to make orderly change possible. Now all three of these institutions, and the values formerly taught in them, are questioned and criticized.

3. Family life has changed. Some children have only one parent. Some children see their grandparents, but others have never seen all their relatives.

4. Violence has become a way of life. Long ago, violence was something that happened to someone else in some other place. Now violence is on TV, in the newspapers, in some children's books, and perhaps lurks in a child's neighborhood. How does the child's attitude about violence affect your teaching?

5. Children face other changes in the world. Someone has said that children now live in a multicolored world—black, white, brown, red, and yellow. Sex roles have changed. Many mothers work outside the home and many fathers accept more responsibility for child care. Many occupations are no longer defined as "women's work" or "men's work."

6. The child's world is getting bigger through technological advances. Because children are seeing more of the world, teachers should not assume what a child knows or has experienced.

7. There is a knowledge explosion. Information in every area is being amassed at such a rapid rate that it is impossible for one person to know everything about anything. Today's child is not expected to store up all the information available. Can you see how this concept influences a child's attitude toward memorizing Scripture?

We cannot grow up in the world of today's children, but we can try to understand them and the world in which they are growing up. Actually each child is born into a particular world that is very different from the world of anyone else. The first child lives in a different world from that of the brother or sister born a few years later.

But, there are some things about children which have not changed. Perhaps physical development is one most easily recognized. The pattern of physical growth remains the same—most children crawl before walking; lose baby teeth before acquiring permanent teeth; and develop large muscle control before perfecting small muscle skills.

## How do you react to your children's needs?

After examining the seven areas mentioned in the preceding paragraphs, you have some ideas about why children are different. Have you been able to identify problems some of your children may have?

You may want to find out more about your children with some simple activities. Ask your students to list three things which they "worry" about the most. They need not sign their names. You may want to introduce some of these problems in future classes. Ask, "What should a child do who is afraid of some older kids at school?" Do you settle for "pray" as the only answer. Yes, children do need to pray and depend on the Lord, but perhaps some child will make other suggestions. One first-grader won over the school bully by telling him he liked the boy and thought he drew "good pictures." Sometimes children can help each other with their problems.

Suggest possible problem situations and let the children tell how the situations would be solved in their own homes. For example, "Your father says there's not enough money to buy both you and your sister new dresses. How do you think your family would solve the problem?" Often your Sunday School lessons will present decision-making activities. Use them. Go slow in telling children what they should do, but listen carefully to see what they say they will do.

## How do Primaries grow?

A child's growth cannot be speeded up or slowed down. Teachers should remind themselves that some things happen—or change—

only as a child grows. Sometimes children recognize this maturity themselves. A third-grader said, "I used to be afraid of monsters, but now I'm not."

Now take a look at the children you teach. See them as individuals and apply age characteristics to them as persons. Remember that every child is in the process of becoming. The six-year-old is becoming seven. He is a very different child in May from what he was the preceding September. In other words, anticipate change throughout the year.

Primaries are people learning to read. They are entering the gateway to a whole new world. Notice how well or poorly your children read; then adjust your teaching. If you have competent readers, let them read Bible verses occasionally.

A Primary's reasoning power is limited, but his imagination is active. He wants to please, but he must wiggle because his muscles cry out for movement. He remembers what he *does* more than what he sees or hears. Good teachers will recognize the need and provide as many purposeful activities as possible. He believes what he is told. Because he has not had much experience in living, the present is most important to him.

*Are you teaching sixes?* If you are, you know that these children are very active. They want to be cooperative, but have difficulties with words, concepts, and generalizations. Here are a few words that some Primaries could not explain: maybe, able, less, and believe. "Every man shall give as he is able" (Deut. 16:17) would not be understood by these children. If you realize the word was not understood, how would you explain the verse?

*Are sevens like sixes?* Yes, in some ways, but they are more settled and perhaps better behaved. These children often dawdle. They are easily frustrated because they seek perfection. Sevens are more group-conscious than sixes; they still like to sit next to the teacher or do things for him. Sevens are more critical and are beginning to evaluate their own behavior. They worry about being late for school, meeting new people, and not getting things done on time. Do not set impossible standards, but anticipate that in their desire for perfection, sevens may work more slowly than either sixes or eights.

*Are eights "big" children?* Eights are not little children, but they are not big children either. They resent being treated as little children, but physical and emotional maturity is still a long way off. By now there is also some resentment of the opposite sex. Organized games are for eights because these children work well in groups. Eights are more reasonable than sevens; they are ready to accept the fact that not everyone can do the same things well. Eights have fewer fears than sevens, but you must listen well to discover the real problems of eights.

Primaries are ready for almost all the basic truths of Scripture if they are presented on their level and related to their lives. A Primary can learn that he has a personal responsibility to God; he can feel secure in God's love and forgiveness. He can understand that God sent His Son to be the Saviour. At six, seven, or eight, many children are ready to receive the Lord Jesus Christ as Saviour.

In understanding children, as in every other area of Christian living, we turn to the Lord Jesus. He, who knows the intent of every human heart and its needs, says, "He that abideth in Me, and I in him, the same bringeth forth much fruit; for without Me ye can do nothing" (John 15:5). Yes, the Lord promises fruit—Christian pupils growing in knowledge and behavior. But He also says we cannot produce this "fruit" without Him. Depend on Him to help you understand the boys and girls you teach!

# To think about

1. What experience have you had in listening to children? How did it help you?

2. Make two lists titled "How it was" and "Now." Draw some comparisons between your childhood and that of some of the Primaries you teach.

3. What do you think is the most important thing any teacher can do for a child?

# 3
# How Do
# Children Learn?

God has created people to learn in many ways. In Old Testament times children learned from their parents' example as well as by hearing God's Word.

"O Israel, listen: Jehovah is our God, Jehovah alone. You must love Him with *all* your heart, soul, and might. And you must think constantly about these commandments I am giving you today. You must teach them to your children and talk about them when you are at home or out for a walk; at bedtime and the first thing in the morning. Tie them on your finger, wear them on your forehead, and write them on the doorposts of your house!" (Deut. 6:4-8, LB)

Because Bible-time children spent a great deal of time with their parents, the children could see, hear, and imitate godly principles. The Hebrew pattern for transmitting values and beliefs consisted in passing them on from one generation to the next. Parents can still help children learn by seeing, hearing, and imitating as parents consistently model godly principles, but our modern society and technology have made it more difficult. How can we help today's child learn to know God intimately, believe on His Son for salvation, and desire to grow spiritually?

Along with others in the local body of believers, the Sunday School teacher has a significant part. From parents' teaching, following the Old Testament pattern, children learn informally. In the structure of Sunday School, children learn formally. It is this latter learning with which we must concern ourselves as we have little or no control over the informal learning that takes place at home.

The Christian teacher needs to know how children learn in order to teach effectively. In Chapter 2 you read that you are teaching the whole child—that what happens to a child *outside* Sunday School affects his or her attitudes and behavior in your class. In addition to this information, you will want to know specific ways in which you may help children experience Bible truth. Because the Bible contains factual information and abstract concepts, it is important to understand children's mental development and thought processes. Children do think differently than adults. A teacher works in partnership with God through the ministry of the Holy Spirit. If the teacher is aware of the work of the Holy Spirit and also understands how children learn, he will better understand how to teach. Remember, you have not taught till the learner has learned. After the teacher realizes that it is the Holy Spirit who makes truth come alive for children, he needs to understand how children think and how he can prepare to teach them.

## What are "levels of learning"?

A child's physical growth follows a natural pattern and so does his mental development. The work of Jean Piaget, child psychologist who worked with children for more than 50 years, is especially helpful to Sunday School teachers. Understanding Piaget's four levels of learning helps adults approach children more sensitively and realistically. Often it is a child's intellectual immaturity and not some perversity that leads to undesirable behavior.

Jean Piaget has considered learning in four distinct but sometimes overlapping stages. He has defined these in terms of chronological age.

1. *Sensory-motor period* (birth to 2 years)

The child learns at this level through his senses and his ability to manipulate objects. In the early years this touch-hear-see method is a child's chief means of learning. But because a child continues to learn in these ways throughout childhood, you will find that Primaries still need to touch and handle.

The next three levels of learning are called "operational." Think of "operational" as meaning that a person can perform an action mentally without physical action. For example, in a frequently described experiment, an adult can recognize that the amount of liquid is the same in a wide jar and a tall vase. However, a young child usually assumes that there is more liquid in the vase because it is taller.

2. *Preoperational thought* (2 to 7)

The child in this period is not able to use certain mental operations which are necessary for mature reasoning and understanding. He has difficulty believing that an object can have more than one property. At this age a child makes judgments in terms of how things *look* rather than on the basis of his mental operations.

Do you better understand why Primaries have difficulty in explaining that God is everywhere? Some children think God is present only in certain places or during specific experiences, such as church, or at bedtime.

3. *Concrete operations* (7 to 11)

Most Primaries are learning at this level, though they are still using some of the processes of earlier years—sensory and preoperational thought. Now the child can manipulate data mentally. He can come to some logical conclusions. He can define, compare, and contrast. He thinks, however, in very concrete terms. Primaries are not the age-group to teach with symbolism. These children need to understand Jesus as the Son of God who became a Man, not how He is the Light, Door, Bread, and Morning Star. Concentrate on literal explanations of biblical events. Leave "There Is a Fountain Filled with Blood" and similar songs till later years when their imagery and symbolism can be understood and appreciated.

Unfortunately, many object lessons, chalk talks, and messages for children count on a child's being able to think abstractly. For example, a dedicated teacher presented an object lesson to Primaries, explaining that a Christian was like a boat whose cargo of sin had been tossed overboard. One of the older Primaries said, "I never knew Jesus put my sins in a brown bag and took them to the bottom of the ocean. So that's where they are." A teacher cannot be too careful in avoiding symbolism with Primary children. Words should mean what they say and say what they mean!

4. *Formal operations* (begins at 11 or 12)

In this period a child can think in abstract terms and can foresee results. He can understand some religious symbolism and appreciate the beauty of some of the figurative language used throughout the Bible.

When a teacher has grasped the significance of the levels of learning, he understands the mistakes children can make in their reasoning. A child cannot understand a Bible truth unless he has the ability to receive it.

There are no shortcuts in teaching logical thinking! When teachers present object lessons, hymns, or other symbolical teaching and believe children understand because they are quiet or parrot the words, those teachers do not realize that telling is not teaching, nor is repeating words really learning. Children must see a truth, understand it, and be able to apply it to themselves before true learning has taken place.

## How can you help Primaries learn?

Adults often seem to be delighted to sit quietly and think, listen, or discuss, but not Primaries! These children need action, and you can give it to them with stories suited to their attention spans; questions that make them think; and learning activities that demand seeing, hearing, bodily movement, and total involvement.

Does this mean that every Sunday School lesson must be packed with action, rushing from one activity to the next? No! Your Sunday School lesson must be based on the Bible, glorify Jesus Christ, and meet the needs of the pupil. You must be aware that Primaries need movement, words they understand, and opportunities to relate Bible truth to their lives. You will provide opportunities to use as many of their five senses as possible. But most important you will prepare your lessons to follow a learning process known as *Guided Discovery Learning*. You will help children learn through discovery. You will guide them because you have a limited time in Sunday School and must define some limitations for their participation or discovery. You will recognize that the learning process is centered in the learner. Unless a child learns, your words and visuals, and any other methods you use, are in vain.

The Guided Discovery Learning process involves three definite steps, often referred to as a learning cycle. This cycle is easily seen in the Bible study and application of a Sunday School lesson. But it is also repeated anytime a child encounters some new knowledge or experience. Here's how it works with a new experience at a learning center. A child comes to a learning center where a model is on display. "What is it?" he asks as he *focuses* attention. He *discovers* what it is by asking a teacher. Then the child *responds* by picking up the model— perhaps a Hebrew scroll—and handling it.

Let's examine the three steps more closely to see how it applies to the Bible study section of a Sunday School lesson.

FOCUS—You begin with a need that is common to Primaries.

Perhaps it is a question, "Do you think kings are always brave?" Or, "How can we be kind?" Another example might be, "Jeff told his mother he'd set the table, but he turned on the TV instead. Jeff didn't obey his mother. Do you think Bible-time people always obeyed?" The FOCUS part of a Sunday School lesson relates to the aim by pointing out a need. For example, the aim may be "That the child will want to show his love for the Lord by being kind." Do you see how the focus question relates to the aim?

Sometimes a learning center will direct a child's attention to the aim of the lesson. Perhaps the Hebrew scroll at the learning center previously described may be used to focus a child's attention on the Bible. The aim of the lesson may relate to how God has preserved His Word. In the lesson about being brave, a child could come to a learning center where he is asked to help compile a list of ways to be brave.

DISCOVER is the next step in the learning cycle. What does God say in His Word about the problem or need? Can you choose a Bible story to go with the focus question, "How can we be kind?" Would it be the story of Dorcas, Ruth, or the Good Samaritan? The Bible story guides children to discover God's answer. Sometimes children help tell the story. You may use pictures, the flannelboard, a filmstrip, an audio tape or videotape, or tell the story yourself. The Bible story helps a child see and hear God's answer to his need. It may bring him to the place where he is ready to *respond* to the Bible truth in his attitude and behavior.

RESPOND is the last step in the learning cycle and confronts the learner with what he should do. Every teacher should bring learners to the point where they want to respond and can see how they can respond. *They should see this for themselves!* If you conclude the lesson on the Good Samaritan, for example, by saying, "Now children, be kind to your brothers and sisters and your parents this week," you have lost the pupils. Let *them* make personal, and often private, decisions about what they will do. You may want to use role play, discussion, visuals, or assignments in the students' activity books, but *do not* tell children what they should do. As the RESPOND step in the Good Samaritan lesson, you may ask children to play out ways they could be kind, draw a picture of someone they will be kind to this week, phrase a prayer, expressing the need for God's help to be kind in a specific situation. Be sensitive. By all means respect children and their ideas! Then pray that the Holy Spirit will work in their hearts.

How should you teach Primaries? First, keep in mind that you have not taught till children have learned. Does this help you see the importance of listening to children and providing many opportunities for them to express what they have learned? Workbook assignments, composing music or creative writing, skits, and many other ways may help you evaluate what children have learned.

Remember most of all that all of the time you, the teacher, are teaching through your own attitudes toward the Lord and toward the children. Your Primaries will "catch" much that you may not realize you have taught.

# To think about

1. Describe the three steps in the Guided Discovery Learning process. Do you realize that these three steps can be repeated more than once in a Sunday School lesson? Decide how this may be.

2. Why would you hesitate to teach Primaries the Gospel song, *We Have An Anchor?* If you do not know this song, look up another one that abounds with symbolism. Now review Piaget's levels of learning.

3. Review a lesson you have recently taught Primaries. How did you guide them? Involve them? Get feedback from them?

# 4
# How Does Moral Development Relate to Spiritual Growth?

In earlier chapters you read of children's physical and mental growth. According to Jean Piaget's research, people move from infancy to adulthood through *four levels of cognitive learning:* sensory-motor period, preoperational thought, concrete operations, and formal operations. Are there also levels of *moral development?*

Let us be sure to recognize that no one can substitute morality for redemption. That is available only through the shed blood of Jesus Christ. An individual can come into God's family only through personal faith in Jesus Christ as his or her Saviour. But we recognize that all people—Christians and non-Christians—know that there are acts of kindness and acts of hatred, selfishness, and evil.

Why do some people usually do right and others usually do wrong? There is no easy answer. A person's heredity, experience, maturity, and interaction with other people all influence actions. But perhaps the greatest motivation for moral development in an individual's life is his source of authority. For a non-Christian it may be a set of cultural mores or humanistic ethics. For a Christian, the source of authority should be the Lord. Christians should make moral judgments that conform with God's guidelines for living.

In recent years some people have tried to study Piaget's findings and then draw conclusions about moral development. Dr. Lawrence Kohlberg of Harvard University has tried to explore the area of moral development. He began in the late 1950s with a group of 70 boys. Every three years since the beginning of his study, Kohlberg has interviewed these individuals. From this long study and other studies in several different cultures, Kohlberg has identified three levels of moral reasoning. His research indicates that *all* persons work through these levels of development in the same order. Your Primaries are now at one of these levels.

## How moral development influences answers

Kohlberg's work gives us some help as we think about the moral development of Primaries. Suppose you present a problem situation to your class. "Jenny wanted a Snoopy pin like her friend's. She knew her mother had slipped some dollar bills into a desk drawer. Should Jenny take two of them to buy the pin?"

Some child will answer no. A teacher would find it easy to accept that answer—surely it is the right answer. However, the teacher needs to find out why a child said no. Unless the teacher takes time to find out the reasoning behind a child's answer, he or she really does not know much about the child's moral judgment. As Christian teachers, we want to know why children answer as they do. Are they beginning to understand biblical principles and live by them?

Think again of Jenny. She could refuse to take the money for any one of these reasons: "Mother might punish me." "God says not to steal. He might do something to me." "I know Mother's saving the money for a family treat." All of these are good reasons for not taking the money. It is easy for a Sunday School teacher to become so concerned with answers that he or she overlooks the reasoning process. However, it is the reasoning process that causes a child to grow in moral judgment. Both answers and reasoning are important.

Before we look at Kohlberg's levels of moral development, let's be sure we remember that every individual grows in his reasoning ability. Just as it is impossible to accelerate physical growth, so it is impossible to speed up an individual's reasoning ability. And telling a child what to think is of little help! New experiences, mental and physical growth, opportunities to discuss the "why" of answers, and freedom to reason for oneself are all helpful in moral development. But each individual must move at his own pace. Because everyone moves through Level 1 to reach Level 2, we should not think of Level

1 as bad—something to move from as rapidly as possible. It is "good" as long as it meets the individual's reasoning capacity. We may, however, be concerned if a 30-year-old is still making judgments at Level 1: he has not grown in his reasoning ability, but is still experiencing the world within a child's limitations. Kohlberg's levels show us how people progress in moral development, but we must be careful not to grade or judge children or adults.

# Kohlberg's levels of moral development

### The Premoral Level
Kohlberg recognizes that, prior to the age of five or six, a child does not have the thought processes to consider a moral dilemma and make a judgment as to what is right or wrong. It is true that even young Primaries are still learning what is right or wrong by asking parents and teachers. However, as Christians we may believe that some children of five or six have been exposed to biblical principles and therefore can make some moral judgments. In such cases children are reasoning at Level 1.

### Level 1—Preconventional
Children generally move into this level before the age of 10. At this level a person knows many things that are good and others that are bad. However, he focuses his attention on what pain or pleasure will come to him as the result of some action. If Jenny in our example refused to take the money because of punishment, she is reasoning just as many children do. In fact, children often use Level 1 reasoning to define wrong as the things for which they are punished.

At Level 1 moral judgments are based on punishment and pleasure—will I be punished? What's in it for me?

### Level 2—Conventional
Probably most individuals do not reach this level before the age of 10 or 12. Now right is defined as the things good people do. Wrong is what bad people do. Can you see how this level of reasoning is directly related to the child who chooses a hero (or heroine) from sports, or patterns behavior after that of an attractive teenager? In

addition to models or heroes, the individual becomes concerned about rules. "What do the rules say?" Older elementary children are very concerned about rules and justice according to rules as they see them.

As teachers of Primary boys and girls we need to understand both Level 1 and Level 2 reasoning because most of our children will be reasoning at one of these levels. Perhaps you will have some immature Primaries who are still functioning at the Premoral level.

*Wonderful, wonderful Jesus!*
*Who was once a child like me;*
*Wonderful, wonderful Jesus!*
*Like Him I want to be.*

The concept in this song encourages a child to make some choices on the basis of being like Jesus. Teachers cannot move a child to Level 2, but experience with a song like this and discussion as to how one can be like Jesus, help a child experience Level 2 reasoning.

Have you known some young person who turned aside from Christianity because he could not live with the thought of God as a Policeman, ready to enforce punishment? If you have, you may realize that the young person never got beyond Level 1 reasoning in his spiritual life. How important it is for teachers to impress children with the fact that God shows His love, mercy, forgiveness, justice, and patience, as well as His holiness and perfection.

*Level 3—Postconventional*
Some people never reach this level of moral development. If they do, it is seldom before they enter their 20s or 30s. Because this is true, a Primary teacher is not concerned with Level 3 in relation to the children. This level deals with universal principles—right is living by principles which bring about justice for all.

If you are interested in learning more about Kohlberg's levels of moral reasoning, there are a number of helpful books. One is *Patterns in Moral Development,* by Catherine M. Stonehouse. Stonehouse is interested in helping both teachers and parents facilitate Christian moral development.

## Why are we concerned with moral development?

Christian values do not just happen! The Bible does not outline moral development at Kohlberg's levels. But God as the Authority does give principles for life and living that are accepted by Christians through moral reasoning. What can a Primary teacher do to facilitate moral development in his or her pupils?

First, you can take time to ask why a pupil has given a particular answer. Earlier in this book, teachers were told that they must listen. Listen to your pupils to see what moral reasoning they are using. Do not condemn a child who sees God as a huge adult ready to punish, but be sure that the child is hearing from you that God loves him. You will want to help children apply biblical principles through problem situations—moral dilemmas. "What should a person do? Why do you say that?"

Thus far we have been concerned with the process of moral reasoning. However, a child needs content for moral reasoning. In the Bible God has revealed what is right and wrong. He has revealed how people are to live and He sent His Son to be our Example as well as our risen Saviour. Check your Sunday School material to be sure that it is based on the Bible, exalts Jesus Christ, and helps pupils see how they can apply biblical principles to their lives. Then your responsibility may be met through faithful, thorough preparation and plenty of time to listen.

Because you know what God has said and demands, it may be hard for you to let children work through questions. Perhaps you need to realize that what a child figures out for himself, under your guidance, will be much more meaningful to him than any number of "right answers" you tell him. What a child makes his own becomes part of him—something he has truly learned.

## What are your spiritual goals for Primaries?

You want pupils to *see* a Bible truth, *understand* what it means, and *accept* its personal application to them, and *respond* to the Lord with some change in behavior and attitude. You teach to effect change in lives, not to build storehouses of Bible facts. And because you teach for changed lives, you are willing to analyze how children learn (Chapter 3). You are ready to consider the levels of moral development explained in this chapter. Now you need to know what your Primaries can learn.

You want the Bible to become reality for your Primaries. The Bible is for today and it is for real! *Children learn a great deal when they are actively involved in the learning process.* You already know something of how children think and how they use moral reasoning. A later chapter on methods will tell you how to involve the children. The purpose of the following pages in this chapter is to help you discover *what* children can learn.

Your Primaries will learn when you build on their potential—not their limitations. For example, children are limited in their reading ability and logical thinking. But a Primary's potential may be expressed in this statement: "The Primary child is God-inclined, with a tender conscience, a strong impulse to obey, and implicit faith. He still believes what he is told, but is already beginning to seek proof and certainty."*

## What should children know about the Bible?

Do your Primaries understand that the Bible is the Word of God and therefore the basis of Christian faith and its final authority? What recent lessons have helped your children see that Bible truth always applies to daily living? Are your Primaries growing in their love for the Bible? Does your curriculum help children understand the origin of the Bible, including its preparation and preservation? Do your Primaries know something of biblical customs, history, and geography?

Supplemental books, such as a children's Bible picture dictionary, can be useful. An illustrated Bible, flannelboard stories, simple charts, and easy-to-read flash cards also help children learn. You need not buy everything available, but be sure you or your Sunday School invests in enough material to make learning interesting and effective.

If you follow your Sunday School curriculum and if it is true to the Bible, you are teaching the parts of the Bible that trained Christian

---

*J. Omar Brubaker and Robert E. Clark, *Understanding People* (Wheaton, Ill.: Evangelical Teacher Training Association, 1972), p. 38.

educators believe to be suitable for the age. If the curriculum writers seem to be well qualified through personal belief, training, and experience, confidently accept their lesson outlines and follow them, adding only what meets specific needs for your children.

Are you interested in teaching children to memorize Bible verses? Most teachers believe Bible memorization to be important, but most children do not want to memorize. Why? Perhaps the material has little meaning for them. Verses to be memorized should be based on real needs, helping a child choose God's way, or feel confident in His love and care. What suggestions about Bible memorization are in your curriculum guides?

## What should children know about prayer?

What is your goal? Do you want each child to be able to pray naturally and frequently? (Children will better understand if you say that prayer is talking to God.) The children will follow your example in the words they use and also in the ease and frequency of their prayers. How would you describe your prayer life? Is it a good example of what prayer is?

The test of a teacher's ability may be his skill at leading children in prayer. What does a literal-minded Primary think if his teacher prays, "Lord, keep us in the shadow of Thy wing and in the hollow of Thy hand"? The more personally you know your pupils and their interests, the more effectively you can word prayers that meet their individual needs.

You will want to help Primaries understand that often they have some responsibility in working with God to answer their prayers. What is their responsibility in keeping safe and doing good work at school? If the Primary curriculum is to help children accept God's answers as no, yes, or wait, weave these ideas into your discussions about prayer.

Use variety in prayer. Sometimes ask another adult to lead. At other times let the children pray sentence prayers. Silent prayer helps Primaries form the habit of intimate fellowship with God. Prayer poems are useful because the group can pray together. Then too, some families have become more aware of the need for prayer because a child has insisted on praying a prayer poem before meals.

## What should children know about worship?

"Let us worship and bow down;
let us kneel before
the Lord our Maker" (Ps. 95:6).

Does your Sunday School period include *instruction, worship, fellowship,* and *service?* Perhaps it is easier to experience and teach *instruction, fellowship,* and *service* than it is to lead children in genuine *worship.*

What is worship? Going to church? Singing? Giving? Praying? Worship may be defined simply as telling God of His worth—His worthship. Children can understand that worship is praising God for who He is, without asking Him to do something. Worship is love, admiration, awe, reverence, and adoration. No one can worship without having some change in his own spirit. "We cannot have true communion with the high and holy One, the Lord of lords, without some personal reaction. The change starts inwardly and manifests itself outwardly."*

How do children worship? Worship must involve the child in a personal response to God through prayer. It may be aided by Bible verses, songs, giving the offering, and often with audiovisuals that create an atmosphere of reverence, love, and praise. But each child must worship for himself. No one can worship for another.

Individuals can worship the Lord at any time and in any place, but Sunday School superintendents are concerned with group worship. How does this come about? By careful planning! A hit-and-miss collection of Bible quiz questions, memory verses, and action songs does not build toward a worship experience. Children will also worship best with what is familiar and meaningful.

The Primary course should answer children's questions about God and their relationship to Him, His Word, and His Son. It would be easy to list the Christian beliefs that grow out of the Primary course, but it will mean more to you if you work out such an outline for yourself. After you have examined your curriculum materials, you are ready to fill in an expanded outline of the following.

---

*Eleanor Hance, "Teaching Children to Worship and Pray," *Childhood Education in the Church,* (Chicago: Moody Press, 1975), p. 276.

## What should a Primary know about the following subjects?

1. The Bible
2. Sin
3. Salvation
4. God
5. Jesus Christ
6. Prayer
7. Worship
8. Creation
9. Giving and Missions
10. Christian action or standards

# To think about

1. What does a teacher need to do after a child has proposed a solution to a problem situation?

2. Why should Primary teachers be concerned with the moral development of their students?

3. What are some subjects you want to see included in your Primary curriculum?

# 5
# How Will You Organize Your Department?

Every Sunday School has its teachers, rooms, and records, but remember that there can be no Primary Sunday School department without children. Your organization will be based on the children. How many do you have? What percentage are first-graders? Do you have some slow learners? How large should your classes be? What children should be put together?

The younger the children, the more space they need. Primaries need more movement than young teens, so they must have more space. They need inviting rooms that say, "You're welcome and wanted here!" Before you read any further, ask yourself, "How do I let a child know he is an important individual? Is a hook for his coat and a card for his name enough?"

Even more than the room, it is the people a child meets who make Sunday School a good experience. An outstanding teacher once said, "I try to compliment or encourage every child in my class individually each Sunday. I find it does something for them and it does a lot for me!" When you take time to treat each child as an individual, you will never have to ask, "Whatever happened to Jeff McGrew?" because you will miss Jeff the first Sunday he is absent. Recognizing children individually also makes you aware that some come from whole families and others from single-parent homes. You will know if you have children with stepparents, and those who are living with grandparents or in a foster home.

Judy is from a two-parent home, but she has more problems than Jon who lives only with his father. Each of Judy's parents works at two jobs, and she is literally being raised by a teenage sister.

## Keeping records

If you are to know children as individuals, records are important. Your Sunday School supplier has a form which you can use to record a child's name, address, telephone number, birthday, family members, relationship to the church, and perhaps some additional notes about his interests, health, or problems. These records should be your personal property; they do not belong in a desk drawer in the Sunday School room where others have access to them.

The department secretary (or superintendent) needs records too. Names, addresses, telephone numbers, and attendance are important because these records are used for:

1. Knowing who is present and who is absent.
2. Assigning follow-up of absentees. (Don't make a pupil feel guilty because he has missed Sunday School. He may have been absent because of illness or the unwillingness of another family member to bring him.)
3. Seeing department growth.
4. Ordering supplies.
5. Assigning children to classes.

If you're a department superintendent, you should know every child by name. If there are more children than you can easily recall, perhaps you have too many pupils in your department. How many Primaries can study, worship, and work effectively in a group? The following chart may be helpful to you.

| Number of pupils in grades 1-3 | up to 45 | 46-90 | 91-120 | 121-160 |
|---|---|---|---|---|
| Number of departments needed | 1 | 2 | 3 | 4 |

The chart allows for the maximum number of pupils. Actually, when you have 20 or more Primaries who are in one grade at school, try to organize a separate department. Children learn better in smaller groups—and an overcrowded room invites misbehavior.

## Is discipline a problem?

The subject of discipline is related to many of the statements in this book and has not been treated in a separate chapter. For example, if you do not understand that Primary children think very concretely, you may be talking above their heads. Naturally this leads to lack of attention which results in physical action—pinching, poking, pushing, talking, etc. Any teacher whose children consistently misbehave should look at a number of factors:

1. Have you really prepared to teach your children where they are? Preparation should include daily prayer for each pupil.
2. Is the room comfortable? Too hot or cold? Too dark or does the sun shine in their faces? Enough space? What about the color and any wall decorations?
3. Are the children's personalities suitable? What problems might arise if you place a child with a learning disability in a group of gifted children? Are there some immature children who set out to upset one another? (If so, they should be separated in class or moved to a different teacher.)
4. Does your lesson move and really involve the children?

Generally, small classes of five to eight children are ideal because in a small group a pupil feels that he belongs. The teacher is also able to sense individual needs and use methods that involve every child.

Many teachers do not understand that discipline is not punishment for wrong action. See if you can accept this definition of discipline: "Discipline is guiding a child to become self-controlled." Perhaps you need to ask yourself some of these questions:

1. What is the child doing that is disruptive and what is he disrupting? Evaluate what you are doing and saying.
2. Why is the child doing this? Some reasons may include: for attention, to test or manipulate the adult or out of his own frustration. If a child is looking for attention, explain that his behavior does not help the class work together. Try not to condemn him as an individual.

3. What am I going to do about it? If you let a child continue to disrupt the learning of other children, you are penalizing them. Decide what you are going to do about the disruptive child. Discover what is behind his behavior. Try to help a child conform. Which is better? "David, if you wiggle so much, you'll have to move." Or, "David, if you want to hear the story, you'll need to keep quiet." Try to place responsibility on the child and for a reason. "You can see better if you sit here," etc.

The average Sunday School teacher is not trained in diagnosing behavioral problems, but there is something you can do. Talk with the child's parents; discover where the child is going to school. Then find what is "good" behavior at school. You may want to talk with the school teacher as well.

Tim caused havoc in the Primary Department. He pushed, pinched, jumped on the back of another child, and hid under the table. But with a teacher on a one-to-one basis, he was likable and interested. The Primary staff did not know what to do! One day his mother brought Tim to Sunday School. As the superintendent talked with her she asked, "Where does Tim go to school?" "Oh," replied the mother, "you've noticed!" and she named the school. The superintendent realized then that this child was attending special education classes and naturally found the standard in the Primary Department very frustrating. She complimented the mother on the child's good points and immediately resolved that Tim would have to be taught on a one-to-one basis.

## Making the most of space

Few Sunday Schools have ideal arrangements, but most Sunday Schools can make better use of the space they do have. Here are a few tips to make even poor space more usable.

1. Omit noisy activities if the acoustics are poor. The children may move, but they do not need to march or play in a rhythm band. They should never run to their classes.

2. If dismissal time or periods when children regroup are noisy times, consider other methods. For example, dismiss all the children with blue eyes, brown shoes, or red in their clothing. Or call the children by name, or dismiss them by class.

3. Any room is a better room when all teachers are "on deck."

4. Proper ventilation is a must for any room.

5. Avoid a last-minute scramble for materials—be prepared.

6. If more than one class must meet in the same area, try to have at least three classes meet in that area. When children must listen to two competing voices, they can be easily distracted by a second voice. But when three or more classes meet in the same area, it is much harder for children to follow the sounds and activities of two other classes.

7. Remove any unnecessary furniture. If you have adequate floor covering—tile or carpet—your Primaries can spend part of the time sitting on the floor. Then provide tables and chairs for some activities. Or you may ask the children to carry their chairs from place to place.

## A checklist for your department

1. Windows: If your room is below ground level, cover the window panes with self-adhesive paper or attractive curtains. It is frustrating and distracting to see feet and automobile wheels outside. Do the windows need curtains? Can parents be enlisted to make them? Are the windows clean? Can you use window panes to display seasonal decorations: leaves, flowers, birds, pumpkins, snowflakes?

2. Floors: Is the covering durable and attractive? A concrete floor can be painted, but perhaps the most satisfactory covering is carpeting. Should this be a long-range goal for your department?

3. Storage: Is there adequate space to hang outer clothing and store art materials, seasonal decorations, song charts, and audio-visuals?

4. Walls: Are you satisfied with them? How can they be improved? Bulletin boards, picture rails, and chalkboards help make a room more attractive and usable.

5. Tables and chairs: The best chairs for Primary children have seats 14 inches from the floor. Tabletops should be about 10 inches higher than the chair seats.

## Worshiping

Worship is feeling near to God, recognizing His worthship, and responding to Him in love and praise. Every teacher should recognize that his own attitude and spirit are important in setting the departmental mood for the worship service.

God has commanded worship (Ps. 96:8-9). Not to worship is to disobey God. Do you know that you are partially responsible for your Primaries' worship experiences?

Should worship begin or end the Sunday School hour? When Sunday School begins with worship, stragglers can slip into the group easily. Sometimes a pianist must be shared with another department. Perhaps a room large enough for all the Primaries to gather together is not available later in the hour. Does this justify, however, scheduling worship at the beginning? There may be practical considerations for having worship first, but whenever possible, Primaries should be helped to worship *after* Bible study. Then they are worshiping or responding to God on the basis of what they have learned. When worship begins the hour, the superintendent is handicapped because he cannot involve pupils in responding to God on the basis of class experience.

Do the worship services in your Primary curriculum provide for meaningful worship experiences? They do if:

1. There is a central theme correlated with the Bible study for the lesson.

2. The service provides opportunity for children to participate: holding visuals, reading Scripture, taking the offering, etc.

3. There is variety in the services. Worship should not follow a set routine.

4. The service leads to a climax, offering the worshipers an opportunity to respond.

## Working as a team

Each worker in the Primary Department has one or more specific responsibilites, but perhaps the greatest responsibility is to work with each other as a team! Do you pray for one another? Share prayer requests? Can you rejoice in God's answers to prayer in your own lives? Is the atmosphere of the department charged with love—or is the atmosphere tense and nervous? If the unexpected turns up, are you sympathetic to one another's needs? Do you criticize one another's lifestyles or teaching methods?

If our own love is fervent
and not just words,
If we have prayed through
and not just prayed,
If we expect God to work
and really change things,
If we've prepared thoroughly
not just read "our lesson,"
If we're ready to go the "second mile"
and do the extras,
Then the emotional climate of our room
will reflect the Lord Himself.

The Primary superintendent should feel responsible to develop a team caring-sharing spirit, but it is also the responsibility of every teacher to work together for a team spirit that the children can feel. If teachers are overflowing with God's grace, His Spirit is free to produce the love of God. Then we find children responding spontaneously; we discover ourselves getting thrilling new ideas; and the entire department will grow in love for the Lord and for one another.

# To think about

1. Why would the children in your class think that they are important to you? What else could you do?

2. Why are records important? What ones do you keep?

3. Why is discipline or a standard of behavior important? How are you helping children become self-controlled?

4. How could your room or your department be made more attractive?

# 6
# How Will
# You Teach?

You want the Bible to become reality for your Primaries. The Bible is for today and it is for real! If children think of the Bible as a collection of old stories, interesting but often impossible, how will they respond to its teachings? Your methods are important. What ones are best for Primaries?

You will want to teach in the ways that Primaries learn best. Perhaps a review of Chapter 3 will be helpful. Then you'll think of ways that children learn through *seeing*—pictures, maps, films, chalkboards, etc.; by *hearing*—stories, music, records, and tapes, people sharing experiences, singing, reading, and talking. Of course, *doing* is particularly important—art, creative writing, role play, and simple research. Children learn in a variety of ways, and at different rates of speed.

Some methods of teaching are old, such as storytelling, but others are very new, including use of video cassettes. Any method you use should be related to the content you want to teach and the people who are to learn—your students. Look at them again—see whole children. Are some calm and controlled? Do some have visual and hearing disabilites? What emotional problems may some children have? Do you have any who are hyperactive?

## What methods are you using?
Primaries want to *do*. Check the following two lists to see what your

children do and what you as a teacher do. If these lists are not complete, add your other activities.

| What children do | What teachers do |
|---|---|
| Record on tape | Tell stories |
| Sing | Lead singing |
| Read | Read |
| Role play | Show filmstrips |
| Hold visuals or | Prepare all visuals |
| manipulate them | and use them |
| Answer questions | Talk, TALK, TALK |
| Talk | Pray |
| Ask questions | Listen to children |
| Pray | Ask questions |
| Work on assignments | Tell a great deal |
| Look at teacher's visuals | |
| Take offering | |
| Celebrate birthdays | |
| Write or draw | |
| Compose music | |
| Discuss | |
| Learn Scripture | |
| Listen to teachers—80% of the time | |

Which list has more checks? What are some things you never let children do? Are your children doing as much as they can? If not, what changes can you make to involve Primaries in more activities? Do you see why your children would enjoy Sunday School?

Everything done in Sunday School ought to get *inside* the child. Everything ought to make a child think, feel, or decide to do. Each child should become so involved that he doesn't have time to poke another child, explore the content of pocket or purse, or think up some other way to disturb learning for himself and the group.

## How a child feels
"Our Sunday School is boring. The teachers think you should always listen—even when you don't understand. And if you fool around the

least bit, they think you're forgetting and get mad. Some teachers don't give you anything to think about, or at least they want your answers to be like theirs. I like to have my own ideas.

"But let me tell you about our substitute teacher last week. At first we were going to make it hard for him, but he started talking and we liked what we heard. It was the story about the widow's oil, remember that? We're third-graders so we know the story pretty well. Mr. Baker, the substitute teacher, just asked us to think about the story. He said, 'How come the oil was so important?' Right away we said that crude oil is very important. Were we surprised when we found out it wasn't crude oil. After someone guessed 'olive oil,' Mr. Baker had us look in dictionaries and stuff to see why it was important."

What did Mr. Baker do that was different from this child's previous teacher? He made the children think; he discovered something they didn't know; and he forced them to *do* simple research.

## What methods may be effective with your children?

There are no simple answers. Think about your children and the methods you are willing to try. Try to use at least three different methods in each lesson.

Children learn through their senses and their curiosity. Is this how you teach? What is there for children to see, handle, or hear in Sunday School? Is there anything in the room that arouses curiosity?

What do your Primaries find when they arrive? Activity centers, such as music, art, reading, or writing, can offer a variety of opportunities to the children. Do you have a nature center during some seasons of the year? Is it kept up-to-date with a magnifying glass and interesting books or pictures? Is there a place to talk with a teacher about memory verses and try learning or repeating them? Do you provide games to help in learning Bible verses?

No teacher can reasonably expect to use the same method or methods each Sunday. Of course, it takes less time just to go through the same routine each week, but time spent in preparation is well-rewarded with the eager attention and changed lives of the children. A few of the methods are briefly described here.

*Storytelling* is an excellent method for Primaries, but it can be overworked. Every story should have four major parts: introduction, body, climax, and conclusion. Do the stories in your teaching material have this structure? The introduction should be brief, setting the stage and plunging into the action. The body is the longest part of the story, and, for Primaries, should be action-oriented. Long descriptions are not interesting to Primaries, but they enjoy dialogue. The climax marks the pinnacle of action and reveals the "why" of the story. The conclusion should be short, tying all the ends together. *Do not* tell the children what the story means. The story should make its own point, though at times you may ask, "What is the story saying to us?"

*Story playing* is frequently overlooked. Playing out the story may often be the creative expression necessary to complete the learning process. Story playing may take the form of puppets, role playing, pantomiming, finger plays, or simple dramatizations. The main purpose of story play is to help a child "get inside the skin" of another person and feel the story.

*Visual aids* come in a variety of forms and sizes. Some are better than others. Here are a few standards to use in evaluating visual aids:

1. Are they biblically authentic?
2. Are they attractive and up-to-date?
3. Are they correlated with the material?
4. Are they necessary to the lesson?

Visual aids include flannelboards, chalkboards, pocket charts, overhead projectors, flat pictures, posters, simple charts, flashcards, filmstrips, slides, models, dioramas, videotapes, and objects.

Some Sunday School curriculums provide teaching resource packets for teachers and superintendents. These, as well as correlated Bible teaching pictures, are a worthwhile investment. Remember, you are teaching for eternity. Think of all the audiovisual "garbage" your children see and hear elsewhere! Your teaching can counteract this as well as instill new ideas.

*Music* helps children praise the Lord, but songs also help them express other feelings as well. Music is a means of involving the children at a personal level, so songs should be chosen with care. Sunday School curriculum writers usually select music to be used with the lessons, but if you choose your own songs, you will want to check their rhythm, length of phrases, pitch range, melody and harmony, tempo, tone quality, and style. Children may enjoy a song because they can clap, whistle, and move to the rhythm, or because they like the jingle-jangle of the words. But these things alone are not worthy reasons for teaching a song. Here are some tests to use in selecting an appropriate song:

1. Is it correlated with the lesson or unit aim?
2. Are the words consistent with Scripture?
3. Are the words emphasizing important truths or are they merely rhythmic and pleasing?
4. Are the words interesting and clear—free from symbolism?
5. Are the words understandable to Primaries?
6. What does this song encourage the children to do?

*Other creative activities* include writing and art activities. Some children enjoy writing poetry, playing games to learn memory verses, composing music, or practicing choral reading. Art activities may include individual pictures, wall murals or friezes, picture folders, notebooks, posters, banners, etc. Consult your curriculum materials to see what creative activities there are.

Can learning about the Lord be exciting? Can the learning really "stick," make a change in the child's life? Yes! A dedicated, prepared, creative, loving teacher, working in partnership with God, can bring this about. Will you!

# To think about

1. Why may a student be better able than the teacher to evaluate a teaching method?
2. Use the checklist "What children do" to evaluate your next several Sunday School lessons.
3. How can you become a better storyteller?

# 7
# Will the Children Receive Jesus?

Surely you want your Primaries to receive the Lord Jesus as Saviour. This should be the goal of every Primary teacher. Because salvation is so important a matter, this entire chapter will discuss it. Every Primary leader should know how to explain salvation.

Children can understand the significance of Christ's death for them. If they are confused about the wonderful story of salvation, it is probably not the message, but the method or content used in presenting it.

By the time a child reaches Primary years he knows something about right and wrong. He is probably aware of his personal wrongdoing. He may feel the guilt of unforgiven sins and be glad to know he can have his sins forgiven. But we cannot force children to accept Christ. Only the Holy Spirit can bring conviction, and He works through the temperament and the daily circumstances of each child more intimately than we could ever understand.

There is real danger in the belief that children are not old enough to understand salvation. But it is also dangerous for a Sunday School teacher to assume that all children in a group are already Christians. It is his or her responsibility to make clear that Jesus came to be the Saviour from sin for all who believe and put their trust in Him. This does not mean that a teacher will constantly talk about receiving Christ, but it does mean that he will know his pupils and keep in mind that some may not be Christians.

# Negatives to avoid

1. Don't make comments that would cause a Primary to think he belongs to the Lord when he does not. Instead, say, "Many of us love Jesus," "Most of us have asked Jesus to be our Saviour," or "If you love Jesus. . . ."

2. Don't confuse a child with symbolism. Because Primaries think of the literal sense of a word, what might the following expressions mean to a Primary?

"Don't you want a white heart? Give your heart to Jesus."

"Do you want a robe of righteousness?"

"Don't you want Jesus to come into your heart and take out all the sin? He will fill that big empty space."

A classic example of what *not* to say to children is: "Some Holstein cows are nearly all white with a few black spots and others are nearly all black with only a few white spots—just like people. Some are mostly nice with a little bad in them, and others are mostly good, but, 'All have sinned and come short of the glory of God.'"

Whenever you find an appealing story or object lesson, try to look at it from a child's viewpoint. If he takes the application literally, what does it say to him? It is usually safe to follow a curriculum that emphasizes salvation without symbolism.

3. Don't use fear as a motive. It is true that unbelievers will not be with the Lord, but a child who "receives Christ" only because he is afraid may not really know the Lord.

4. Be careful about group invitations, asking the children to stand or come forward. This action is easy for most children. Children like to move, please their teacher, react automatically when spoken to, follow others, and jump to conclusions.

On the other hand, adults like to sit still, please the group, reconsider and make independent decisions, and hesitate because they are self-conscious. We ask adults to do something that is difficult for them, such as coming forward, to show their interest in receiving Christ. When we ask children to do the same thing, and it is something children like to do, we may think their response indicates a personal encounter with the Lord when this is often not the case.

If we want to help a child make a meaningful decision, we should ask him to do something he finds a bit difficult, such as staying after class. When the Holy Spirit is dealing with a child, he will be ready to do something that requires some thought and perhaps patience.

5. Don't reward a child for receiving Christ. Desire for a book, pencil, or some other gift can easily become a substitute for a genuine response.

6. If a child has received Christ, don't use his Christianity to make him "behave." Resorting to "John, Christians don't poke people" would be a sin on the part of a teacher or parent.

## Positives to follow

1. Use a curriculum which suggests songs, Bible verses, discussions, audiovisuals, and stories that help explain salvation at a Primary's level of understanding.

2. Ask a child to do something he would not normally want to do. You may say, "If you want to know how Jesus can be your Saviour, stay after class."

3. Take plenty of time with the child, making sure that he knows why he stayed after class or asked for information. You may ask, "Sarah, why did you stay after class? What did you want to talk about?"

4. Use the Bible, but limit the number of verses you use. Give the child one "assurance" verse that he can understand and remember. If the child has a Bible or a New Testament, underline the verse for him.

5. The following steps can be most helpful in leading a child to Christ:

a. God loves you very much.

b. All people have sinned or done wrong. You have done wrong (Rom. 3:23). Let the child mention some of his sins if he is willing to do so.

c. God loves you so much that He sent His Son to die for you and take the punishment for your sin (John 3:16 or 1 Cor. 15:3-4).

d. If a person believes that Jesus died to take the punishment for his sin, and asks Jesus to be his Saviour, that person can belong to God's family forever (John 1:12). Do you want to ask the Lord to forgive your sin? Do you want Jesus' punishment to count for you? (Some children who have had a substitute teacher at school can be helped by calling Jesus our Substitute.)

e. Ask the child to tell someone else—another teacher or child—what he has done.

f. If the child's parents would welcome knowing of his salvation, talk to them. If a child is likely to face antagonism at home, assure him that you will be praying for him.

g. Later, let a child know that the Lord will not stop loving him or take him out of His family if he does wrong. Be sure the new believer understands that the Lord will forgive when he prays to Him (1 John 1:9).

## A child's spiritual growth

After a child becomes a Christian, you may see some changes in his behavior. You do not see your Primaries every day, so do not be disappointed if the behavioral changes you notice seem slight. You cannot expect perfection from a child any more than you can from an adult. Faithfully pray for the child and depend on the Holy Spirit to guide and direct the child as He knows best. You may see the Spirit work in the lives of the children in your class as He worked in John Johnson's life.

John's parents did not particularly appreciate the handwork he brought home; they did not attend parents' meetings; and neither parent bothered to read take-home papers to John. But it was impossible for them not to notice how John changed. He was more truthful. He tried to help. And he even asked to pray before meals.

Here's how John's father explained what happened. "I never had much time for church, but I surely saw a change in John. And after a while both my wife and I decided to visit the church. We felt if the church could make such big changes in John, there must be something to it. Today I'm a witnessing Christian, and it's really because John went to Sunday School and found Christ!"

# To think about

1. Give examples of what you should avoid in explaining salvation to a Primary.

2. How would you explain Christ as "our Substitute" to a Primary?

3. List three or four Bible verses you would use in explaining salvation to a Primary child. Have you memorized these verses? Why should you?

4. What is your reponsibility to a child after he has received Christ as Saviour?

# 8
# How Will You Prepare a Lesson?

You are engaged in a great and mighty task to be accomplished only with the help of a great and mighty God! Let's look at a definition of Christian education that has been established by the Accrediting Association of Bible Colleges.

"Christian education is the Bible-based, Christ-centered process (1) of leading persons into a transforming experience of truth, ever maturing into the fullness of Christ; and (2) of equipping them by fundamental knowledge, attitudes, and skills to render effective service in the will of God." The definition continues by stating that Christian education is involved with both educational institutions and the local church. Extrachurch or parachurch agencies, such as Awana clubs for children, are also involved. Perhaps you will want to read this definition frequently as you think of your opportunity and responsibility in teaching Primaries.

You, Teacher, are transmitting the truth of God to your children in such a way as to bring about their wholehearted response and obedience to God. Or more simply, you want to bring your boys and girls to Christ, build them up in Christ, and have them live for Him at school, home, and in every experience that comes to them now and in the years ahead.

Is lesson preparation important in the light of this responsibility? Are tools important? Have you been thinking that pictures, visual aids, handwork, and worksheets or activity books are too much work or too expensive? Important work requires the best of you and the best of materials.

Your effectiveness as a Sunday School teacher does not come about by accident. First of all, you should be teaching lessons that are Bible-centered because the Bible is God's revelation to man. You and your pupils need to know what God has revealed in His Word. However, you will want to draw life-changing truths from God's Word and teach them in attention-holding lessons to cause children to respond to the Lord. Reaching this goal requires knowledge of the children, saturation in God's Word, careful planning, and prayerful and loving preparation.

## Are you ready?

You want to use Guided Discovery Learning and the learning cycle: *focus, discover,* and *respond.* Do you need to review Chapter 3? This learning cycle will be repeated several times in each week's lesson. Look for it by reading all of the lesson—from beginning learning activities to the end of the printed lesson. How many times did you find the learning cycle?

Now you are ready to look at the total lesson structure. What is the lesson aim? Does your material define how children are to *know* and *feel?* This may not be spelled out, but look till you can write three statements about the lesson:

1. My children are to know how God helped Daniel?
2. My children are to feel (and know) something of God's power.
3. My children should want to pray to God faithfully as Daniel did.

Do you see how these three ideas tie together and actually lead through the learning cycle? Children *focus* on Daniel's problem, *discover* what God did, and want to *respond* to a loving, powerful God. You've realized that the Bible content relates to the aim, but do any of the other suggested activities? Do early learning activities have anything to do with prayer? Is the story or message for the worship period related to prayer, or does it emphasize giving or missions?

Every part of a Sunday School lesson should be related to one aim. This makes for a strong lesson because children's attention is centered on the aim. You have not introduced other ideas that draw their attention to a variety of subjects or aims. If your lesson materials concentrate on one aim, you will be able to achieve *total hour teaching.* The entire Sunday School hour or period reinforces the aim and brings students to a point of decision: "How am I going to respond to what I have learned?"

Sunday School lessons for Primaries should be organized into units of two or more lessons—each unit deals with a single question or theme. Individual lessons are steps toward answering the unit question.

|  |  |
|---|---|
| *Unit:* | How does Jesus want His followers to grow? |
| *1st lesson:* | To consider others |
| | "The Good Samaritan"—Luke 10:25-37 |
| *2nd lesson:* | To pray sincerely |
| | "Jesus teaches how to pray"—Matthew 6:9-13 |
| *3rd lesson:* | To give with love for the Lord |
| | "A gift that pleased Jesus"—Luke 21:1-4 |

You should always be aware of the unit structure, but focus attention on one aim at a time. Each lesson is another step in answering the unit question.

If you have not really thought about the relationship of units to lessons, begin by writing out the aim for the unit you are now teaching. Next list the aim of each lesson in the unit. Do the aims all tie together? Think of ways to illustrate the aims. For example, "To consider others" might mean more to your pupils if you call attention

to their behavior at the drinking fountain. (Primaries are not always ready to take turns or help younger children get drinks.)

Now you are ready to prepare a chart for each lesson. Head your chart with three big organizational questions: "What?" "How?" and "Why?" Fill in your lesson plan under these headings.

| WHAT | | HOW? | WHY? |
|---|---|---|---|
| *Bible content* | *Aim* | *Activities* | *Purpose* |
| God gives His Word to Moses (Ex. 19:1-19; 20:1-21; 24:3, 7, 12, 18; 31:18; 32:15-16) | To know and obey some rules from God's Word | Bulletin board | Establish authority of Bible |
| | | Approach: Why do we need rules? | Introduce purpose of study |
| | | Bible story | Know some of God's rules |
| | | Visuals 10-11 | Visualize event Application |
| | | | Opportunity for response |
| | | Workbook, pages 8-9 | Practice and reinforcement |

As you prepare a chart for each lesson, you will begin to see the importance of the activities suggested in the curriculum. The Bible event is the basis of your teaching, but the activities bring the Bible truth to the pupil in a personal way.

The practice and reinforcement of the lesson aim links Bible learning to life. This is reality-centered teaching, and it follows the easy and educationally sound learning cycle: *focus, discover, respond.* In every lesson you prepare, think of *focus, discover,* and *respond.* You are the children's guide through this learning cycle. Remember, of course, that only the Holy Spirit can bring about a genuine and lasting response to God.

Suppose your children discover through the story of the Good Samaritan that they are to consider others. Now they need an opportunity to apply this newly-learned principle. Role playing, handwork, or an assignment in the workbook will help children see exactly how they can be kind to others. After you have started pupils' thinking, be sure to allow opportunity for their own ideas.

If you are the superintendent, responsible for learning center activities and worship, you should also make a chart. See how the learning activities relate to the lesson aim. Sometimes these may reinforce Bible knowledge—with story reviews and memory verse games. Occasionally the children may be introduced to a new song which they practice for the worship period.

Carefully examine the purpose of all large-group activities. Do the songs reinforce the aim for the day? Assume your study is on Daniel with the aims suggested earlier. Will you choose songs about prayer or salvation? Is your feature for the worship time to be about prayer, or giving to missionaries?

If you are responsible for worship with your Primaries, remember that your purpose is to lead the children to worship and praise God and also make a further response to God on the basis of what they have learned in class. Select stories, songs, Scripture, and other activities which emphasize the lesson aim and correlate with what teachers have done or will be doing. Do not duplicate their efforts. For example, if a worship service precedes classes, you should never tell the Bible story or make its application to life.

The lives of your pupils will be changed if you concentrate on one aim for each Sunday. If you relate all activities to a single theme, your teaching cannot help but make that aim a reality in the lives of your pupils.

## Get set!

These preparation pointers should help you.

1. *Study the pupil's workbook and complete the assignments.* The workbook, used after the lesson presentation, provides an immediate opportunity to apply the lesson.

2. *Plan to ask meaningful questions.* Avoid questions that require little thought and one-word answers, such as "yes," "no," "Jesus,"

"God," "the Bible." Ask "why" and "how" questions to make your pupils think. Challenge advanced pupils with difficult questions; expect unchurched children to answer easy questions. Try to include all children—the quiet ones as well as the Primaries who always volunteer.

3. *Read the take-home paper.* The correlated storypaper will show how the lesson truth applies to life. Urge the children to read it.

4. *Write out several beginnings for your lesson.* Avoid "Now this week . . ." or "Who remembers what we had last week?" Use a picture, a question, or a short modern-day incident to emphasize the lesson.

5. *Practice the visual aids ahead of time.*

6. *Plan to let the pupils express what they have learned.* Expression may come through questions, conversation, playing out the story, handwork, or . . .

7. *Tell the Bible story aloud at home.* Notice your vocabulary.

8. *Sometimes plan to read part of the story directly from your Bible.* Older children may find the verses ahead of time and read them at appropriate places in the story.

9. *Schedule your time,* but also prepare to be flexible. Allow time for pupil activities. Don't tell them to hurry; if you do, you will dry up their creativity and stop their thinking processes.

10. Remember, no teacher can be ready to meet his pupils without first meeting God, the One he serves and represents.

> Ask the Lord to make the lesson real in your own life.
>
> Begin lesson preparation early in the week. The lesson will simmer in your mind and you will have time to collect teaching aids.
>
> Concentrate on Bible study. Your understanding Bible truth and relating it to life is most important.
>
> Detail your plan—fill in a chart similar to the one in this chapter.

## What is mastery learning?

Put simply, mastery learning means that every student masters the content of the lesson. This term has been used in secular education and some Christian educators have wondered about its application to Bible learning. Mastery learning, in secular education, places a great deal of responsibility on the individual student. He or she *helps* select what is to be learned and sets goals with the teacher. Later the students are tested to see if they have achieved the goals. Students know that they are to *master* one area of instruction before going on to another. Dr. Benjamin Bloom at the University of Chicago is credited with developing some of the strategies used in mastery learning.

How does mastery learning apply to teaching Sunday School? At present little has been done to apply this technique to the Sunday School student. There are many reasons for this, including: lack of goal-setting by parents, churches, teachers, and children; irregular attendance; shortness of teaching time; inadequacy of teaching materials that that would permit varied individual instruction; and difficulty of relating Bible content to skills as measured in mastery learning.

What can we apply about mastery learning to the Sunday School? Perhaps the pupil involvement is the easiest to weave into our teaching. How do you introduce a new unit? Do you share the unit question, theme, or aim with your students? Let's use the unit question, "How does Jesus want His followers to grow?" You could tell the children that the Bible studies are going to answer this question, but ask what answers they think your class may find. Suggest that you keep a classroom list of what you discover. There may be other ways you can involve the pupils in planning together. Though this is not mastery learning in its full sense, you'll find that sharing with your students may capture their interest and help them learn.

# To think about

1. Write a definition of Christian education and of Sunday School teaching.

2. Look at your teacher's manual. Does the lesson structure involve *total hour teaching?* How could you change it to relate all activities to one lesson aim?

3. Use the three organizational questions: "What?" "How?" and "Why?"to fill in a lesson plan that you will teach.

# 9
# How Are
# You Doing?

"Therefore, my dear brothers, stand firm. Let
nothing move you. Always give yourselves fully to
the work of the Lord, because you know that your
labor in the Lord is not in vain" (1 Cor. 15:58, NIV).

You will not be able to take all the principles in this book, learn them,
and use them in one week. But when you have put all of the principles
into practice, you will find that every Sunday can be a great
experience *with* the Lord and *in* His work.

Most Sunday School teachers know more—or less—about teaching than they think they do. Try this true/false quiz to find out about
yourself.

T     F     1. Though you know about effective teaching methods,
you give in to the temptation to substitute wordiness—a favorite
device of Sunday School teachers.

T     F     2. You know that an attractive bulletin board and
perhaps curtains at the window will create a better climate for
learning, but nobody else fixes up a room either.

T     F     3. You really love your pupils and usually remember to
send birthday cards.

T     F     4. You have visual aids, but you just don't have the time
to prepare them.

T     F     5. You did try role playing—once.

T     F     6. You feel so unappreciated that you hardly have the

heart to go on. Did God—or the superintendent—call you to teach?
T   F    7. You know evaluation of your teaching would help you improve, but you are glad enough to get through the class period.

If you answered *true* to most of these questions, your mornings in the Sunday School classroom may be unexciting, uneventful, unfruitful, and unfulfilling. If you haven't realized it yet, this book can help you discover areas where you can, with God's help, improve and evaluate your teaching.

## Evaluation

Evaluation is a teaching tool often neglected. It is not enough to think through a teaching session with the commendation, "Well, the children were quiet, weren't they?" Silence on the part of the pupils may have helped the teacher talk, but did the children learn?

Perhaps you would like to evaluate your teaching with some of these questions:

1. Was your approach to the Bible study interesting? Why? Did it lead into the lesson? Did it *focus* attention?

2. Did you tell the Bible story well? Did your presentation help pupils *discover* the main point for themselves? Why or why not?

3. Did the children understand and *respond* by accepting the application of Bible truth to life for themselves? How do you know? Did they ask questions? Did you have to explain repeatedly?

4. What did your pupils learn? Bible facts? A biblical truth that they can apply to life?

5. What role did you play? "My class was teacher-dominated when I . . ."

6. Did the session seem to get out of hand? When? Why?

7. What activities were best? Were any of them too easy or too difficult? Were the visual aids helpful?

8. What will you do differently next week?

## More than a Sunday job

If you take your teaching seriously, you are more than a Sunday teacher. What you do Monday through Saturday can determine whether Sunday is the great spiritual experience it can be.

Do you visit your pupils' homes to discover how the home may be reinforcing or negating Sunday School teaching and to discover parental attitudes toward the child and the church?

When did you last have a cookout or a game time in your home for your class or department? Primaries need fun as well as serious teaching. Have you tried a service project with mature Primaries? Children need to discover that there is a great deal they can do to show forth God's love.

Do you constantly depend on the Lord and His Spirit? The Holy Spirit's particular ministry is to take the Word of God and make it an inner experience for the believer. Even though we ask Him to guide our lesson preparation, He seeks to lead us also during the Sunday School hour. If we are sensitive to His leading, He will help us use the children's questions and comments to make the lesson live. He will take the things of Christ and give them meaning for the children— and for us. Then the children do more than answer questions thoughtlessly or repeat words mechanically, for they are having personal experience with the Lord Himself.

Teaching in the Sunday School is a demanding job because you are not teaching someone how to read, or write, or work with his hands. You are teaching people how to become God's children and live all of life for Him!

God bless you, Teacher!

# To think about

1. List three points—standards or questions—you *have* used to decide that "I had a good class."

2. As a result of reading this book, list three questions you *will* ask as you evaluate a teaching session.

3. Throughout this book you have *focused* on the importance of teaching; you have *discovered* some new things about children or teaching; and you have decided or will decide how you plan to *respond*. Write one way you plan to ask the Lord to help you respond to the new information you now have.

# Additional Resources

Allstrom, Elizabeth. *You Can Teach Creatively.* Nashville: Abingdon Press, 1970.

Baker, Dolores, and Rives, Elsie. *Teaching the Bible to Primaries.* Nashville: Convention, 1964.

Barrett, Ethel. *Storytelling—It's Easy.* Los Angeles: Cowman Publications, 1960.

Ginott, Haim. *Teacher and Child.* New York: The Macmillan Company, 1972.

Ginsburg, Herbert, and Opper, Sylvia. *Piaget's Theory of Intellectual Development.* Englewood Cliffs, N.J.: Prentice-Hall, Inc., 1969.

Jenkins, Gladys G.; Schacter, Helen; and Bauer, William W. *These Are Your Children.* 3rd ed. Glenview, Ill.: Scott, Foresman, 1970.

Jones, Elizabeth. *Teaching Primaries Today.* Kansas City: Beacon Hill Press, 1974.

Rives, Elsie, and Sharp, Margaret. *Guiding Children.* Nashville: Convention Press, 1969.

Stonehouse, Catherine M. *Patterns in Moral Development.* Waco, Texas: Word, Inc., 1980.

Tobey, Kathrene M. *Learning and Teaching Through the Senses.* Philadelphia: Westminster Press, 1970.

Ward, Ted. *Values Begin at Home.* Wheaton, Ill.: Scripture Press Publications, Inc., 1979.

Zuck, Roy B., and Clark, Robert E. *Childhood Education in the Church.* Chicago: Moody Press, 1975.